THE DARK PEAK

Roger Redfern

First published in Great Britain in 2011

British Library Cataloguing-in-Publication Data
A CIP record for this title is available from the British Library

ISBN 978 1 906887 15 5

PiXZ Books
Halsgrove House, Ryelands Industrial Estate,
Bagley Road, Wellington, Somerset TA21 9PZ
Tel: 01823 653777
Fax: 01823 216796
email: sales@halsgrove.com

An imprint of Halstar Ltd, part of the Halsgrove group of companies
Information on all Halsgrove titles is available at: www.halsgrove.com

Printed and bound in China by Toppan Leefung Printing Ltd

Contents

The Dark Peak

How to use this book

The Dark Peak is the name given to the high, gritstone territory occupying most of the northern part of the Peak District National Park. The area offers walking of varying standard from easy to challenging, all in magnificent landscapes.

The core of the Dark Peak is the trio of highest uplands — Kinder Scout, Bleaklow and Black Hill. They are broad, heathery and peaty plateaux dissected by attractively wild tributary valleys usually called cloughs. In the larger dales separating these plateaux are many impressive reservoirs which, together with the surrounding mixed and coniferous plantations, add much landscape value here.

Summertime fires, heavy rainfall and tramping feet have had an adverse influence on these exposed tops, especially after this became part of the first British National Park in 1951. Recent action is helping the regeneration of heather, moss, bilberry and cotton grass. This includes the construction of pathways along the most popular walking routes like the Pennine Way Long Distance Footpath across Bleaklow, and the re-seeding of peaty areas where the natural flora had virtually disappeared.

Fascinating routes, short or longer, can be created without wandering far onto the highest, wildest country. Upper Derwent Dale, the Hope Woodlands, and parts of lower Longdendale are most attractive areas that don't involve going far onto the highest ground.

Each route here is graded from Easy to More Challenging with further details of distance, height ascended and the type of terrain covered, so helping the reader to choose a suitable route. The information blocks contain details of distances and heights in both imperial and metric measures.

All the walks are covered by Ordnance Survey Outdoor Leisure Map 1 — "The Peak District — Dark Peak area" though the beginning and ending of Walk 6 (The Wessenden Valley and West Nab) requires Ordnance Survey Outdoor Leisure Map 21 — "South Pennines".

The maps in this book give only outlines of each route. Reference to the OS map will add interest and help avoid going astray.

Always go well equipped, especially on the routes that involve tough terrain and higher altitude. If unsure of fitness try one of the easier routes first ! Not all of the routes described have convenient places providing refreshment so always take some food and drink.

Tell someone where you are going and your expected time of return. And, having checked the weather forecast, only tackle the challenging routes in clear conditions.

Useful websites:

Peak District National Park
www.peakdistrict.gov.uk

Railway travel
www.nationalrail.co.uk

Bus travel
www.transpeak.co.uk

Peak District Tourist Board
www.visitpeakdistrict.com

Peak & Northern Footpaths Society
www.peakandnorthern.org.uk

Gritstone tor on Kinder Scout.

Key to Symbols Used

Level of difficulty:

Easy

Moderate

More Challenging 🍃 🍃 🍃

Map symbols:

🚗	Park & start
———	Tarred Road
- - -	Footpath
– – –	Walk Footpath
	River, stream or brook
■	Building
+	Church
▲	Triangulation pillar or other landmark
🚻	WC
🍴	Refreshments
🍺	Pub

Walk Locations

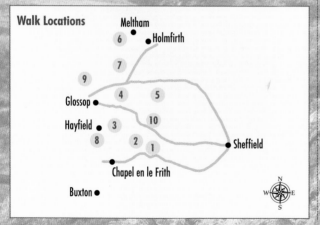

Meltham

6

Holmfirth

7

9

4   5

Glossop

10

Hayfield   3

8   2   1

Sheffield

Chapel en le Frith

Buxton

N
W · E
S

Along the Great Ridge

A high level walk at the head of the Hope Valley.

That great landscape photographer, the late Walt Poucher, christened this high ridge and the title "the Great Ridge" has stuck. It is a watershed barrier separating the western end of the popular Hope Valley from the more dramatic Vale of Edale to the north.

Starting at the eastern end we cross the conspicuous summit of Lose Hill and continue westwards over rugged, shaly Back Tor, traverse the col of Hollins Cross before mounting up to the top of Mam Tor, Peakland's famous "shivering mountain" with its dramatic

Level: ♥ ♥ ♥
Length: 7.5 miles (12 kms)
Ascent: 1,315 feet (400 metres)
Terrain: Steep ascents and descents on the Great Ridge. Otherwise field paths.
Park & Start: Hope village.   GR 173835
Info: Refreshments in Hope and Castleton. Toilets in Castleton.

east face and topped by one of the largest prehistoric earthworks in the area.

Beyond Mam Tor's top the route swings down and through the chaos of the age-old landslip that finally closed the A625 trunk road many years ago. Later the path crosses the stone-walled fields to Castleton, famous for its four show caves and Norman Peveril Castle. Following the path beside Peakshole Water we return to Hope village.

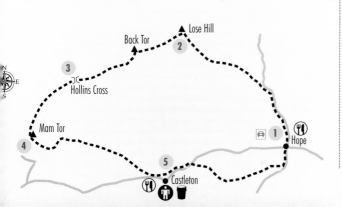

(1) Walk north from Hope parish church, along Edale Road, to Townhead, fork left before the river bridge and the steep path goes up past Losehill End and all the way to the 1,561 feet (476 metres) summit of Lose Hill. A magnificent viewpoint and National Trust property.

(2) Continue south-westwards along the crest of the Great Ridge, over Back Tor and Barker Bank to the col at Hollins Cross.

(3) On again, westwards, and swing up to the summit of Mam Tor, at 1,696 feet (517 metres) the highest point of the walk. The view east down the length of the Hope Valley is magnificent, even when the giant Hope cement works is taken into account.

Back Tor on the Great Ridge.

The summit of Lose Hill, easternmost top of the Great Ridge, was given to the National Trust in recognition of the great achievements of G.H.B. Ward, the famous "King of Ramblers" who had founded the pioneer Sheffield Clarion Ramblers Club in 1900 and continued to fight for the right to roam right up to his death in 1957. The gifted summit area is called "Ward's Piece" in his honour and there's a viewer there highlighting major features visible from the top.

Looking east along the Great Ridge.

Mam Tor from Hollins Cross.

4 Go down the grassy southern slopes to gain the remains of the A625 and either follow it round its notorious hairpin bend or cut down east to pass the rocky defile close to the ancient Odin lead mine. Pick up the footpath that passes Knowlegates Farm and so across the fields to Castleton.

5 Castleton is always busy, a true "honeypot" attracting large numbers of Peak District tourists. Walk along the A625 eastwards through the village and a short way before reaching Spital Bridge take the field path on the right and in less than 1.5 miles (2.5km) reach the public lane close to the pinfold at Hope (originally used to impound straying farm animals). Turn left and soon gain the starting point beside Hope parish church.

Cryer House, Castleton.

Peveril Castle overlooking Castleton.

Odin Mine below Mam Tor's "shivering" east face is reputed to have been worked for lead ore from Saxon (maybe earlier in Roman) times. The earliest known records, though, date from 1663 and it was worked continuously through the 18th century. Across the road from the mine is the dramatic cleft of Odin Gorge, an artificial working where the lead vein has been completely removed.

Collapsed road below Mam Tor.

2 **The Round of Grindsbrook**

On the rocky rim of the Dark Peak's highest ground.

This deep, steep valley on the southern flank of Kinder Scout, highest ground in the Dark Peak, makes a dramatic central feature for a circular mountain walk around it, starting and finishing in Edale village.

Here is the southern terminus of the Pennine Way Long Distance Footpath that ends at Kirk Yetholm, over the border in southern Scotland.

The initial steep pull to the top of Grindslow Knoll is repaid with fairly

Level: 🐾 🐾 🐾
Length: 6 miles (9.5 kms)
Ascent: 1,300 feet (400 metres)
Terrain: Steep ascent and descent. Some rocky ground. Exposed ground in adverse weather.
Park & Start: Edale village. GR 124853
Info: National Park Information Centre in Edale. Refreshments in Edale.

Kinder Scout

Hartshorn

Nether Tor

4

Grindsbrook Clough

5

Ringing Roger

3

Grindslow Knoll

2

Edale

Pennine Way

1

N
W E
S

level going thereafter, right around the craggy head of Grindsbrook Clough with views down to its narrow gritstone steps where the stream plunges after wet weather. Eventually we descend the rocky arête of Ringing Roger and so through the pasture fields that make such a contrast, back to Edale village.

The Vale of Edale from above Jaggers Clough.

1. Park in the car park at the T junction near Edale railway station and walk up through Grindsbrook Booth. At the road head north of Edale church take the path to the left which is the present day line of the Pennine Way. In a short distance fork off right, aiming up the steepening slopes of Grindslow Knoll which towers ahead.

Hay turner at Barber Booth, Edale.

2. A steep pull up Grindslow Knoll's eastern flank to reach the 1,972 feet (601 metres) summit. Grand views out across the Vale of Edale one way and across the lofty plateau of Kinder Scout in the other direction – at 2,088 feet (636 metres) the highest point in the Peak District National Park.

The Woolpacks, Kinder Scout.

Heardman's Plantation below Ringing Roger commemorates the celebrated Peak District rambler Fred Heardman. A pioneer of open access to these high grouse moors he was for many years landlord of both the former Church Hotel and the Nags Head at Edale.

3 Heading north-west skirt around the upper reaches of Grindsbrook Clough before heading due east along the edge of this broad, heathery plateau with wide downward views to the Vale of Edale.

On Ringing Roger in winter.

4　After crossing the head of Golden Clough turn south-east to reach the top of the rocky arête called Ringing Roger.

5　Go down this spine with care to The Nab, a shoulder half way to the valley floor then follow the zigzag path down past Heardman's Plantation. Head south down the path, cross the pastures and so over the little footbridge over the Grinds Brook to enter Grindsbrook Booth and the starting point.

The Hippo Pool, Kinder Scout.

Across Crowden Clough, Kinder Scout.

3 Kinder Reservoir and Kinder Downfall from Hayfield

In the footsteps of pioneering trespassers.

Level: ♥ ♥ ♥
Length: 7.5 miles (12 kms)
Ascent: 1,300 feet (400 metres)
Terrain: Stiff moorland walking. Some rocky ground.
Park & Start: Bowden Bridge Quarry, Hayfield. GR 047869
Info: Visitor Centre, Hayfield. Refreshments in Hayfield.

This is another challenging walk onto Kinder Scout, Peakland's highest upland. It begins on the western side of this gritstone wilderness and climbs in the footsteps of those pioneer ramblers who sought a legitimate right to roam on these grouse moors in the 1930s. This is the place where the infamous "Mass Trespass" took place in 1932, a milestone in the long struggle for access to this magnificent open country.

We look down upon Kinder Reservoir, climb by William Clough and reach the lofty north-western prow of Kinder Scout before circling south, on part of the Pennine Way, to the top of Kinder Downfall (finest waterfall in the Peak District).

The final part of our circuit involves a descent of delightful tilting sheep pastures to the wooded confines at our starting point.

Pennine Way
Ashop Head
William Clough
3
4
Pennine Way
White Brow
2
Kinder Downfall
Kinder Reservoir
Kinder Scout
The Three Knolls
6
5
Pennine Way
Kinder Low
N W E S
Hayfield
1

Gritstone tor on Kinder Scout.

1 Park at the public car park in the old stone quarry at Bowden Bridge a mile east of Hayfield village. Walk north along Kinder Road with the steep, wooded slopes on Kinder Bank to the left.

2 Ascend to White Brow and so enter Access Land before traversing Nab Brow and entering the narrow confines of William Clough. A steady ascent on a small path for more than a mile (2 kms) to reach the watershed at Ashop Head.

3 Turn right onto the Pennine Way and ascend the steep prow to reach the north-western extremity of the Kinder Scout plateau at 1,968 feet (600 metres). Looking away to the north in clear weather

The plaque on the wall of the old quarry at Bowden Bridge, Hayfield was unveiled in April, 1982 as part of the Fiftieth Anniversary Celebration of the Kinder Scout Mass Trespass of April 24th, 1932. It took many years after this historic pre-war event before great areas of the Peakland moors became available for unhindered rambling.

PEAK DISTRICT
& N C FOOTPATHS
SOCIETY

THIS FOOTPATH TO
THE SNAKE INN VIA
WILLIAM CLOUGH &
THE ASHOP VALLEY
DEDICATED FOR EVER
MAY 29 1897

Historic footpath sign at Hayfield.

The River Sett at Hayfield.

Kinder Reservoir and Kinder Downfall from Hayfield

The Cloughs from Jacob's Ladder, Kinder Scout.

you see a broad prospect of vast moorland extending to Higher Shelf Stones, nearest of the several tops of the Bleaklow plateau (see Walk 4).

(4) Follow the route of the Pennine Way as it keeps along the top of the gritstone cargs for 1.5 miles (2.25 kms) to reach the dramatic rock architecture where the Kinder River plunges off the plateau in the famous Downfall. There is good ice climbing here in severe winter conditions. Continue southwards for about half a mile (0.75 km) before taking a small path that drops diagonally from the top of the edge and heads towards the jumbled ground of The Three Knolls and so down to the lower limit of Access Land where we join a path descending from the east.

On Edale Moor, Kinder Scout.

The steep western flank of Kinder Scout (highest area in the Peak District at 2,088 feet – 636 metres) overlooks the Kinder Reservoir at the foot of William Clough. Completed in 1912 it supplies water to Stockport and inundated the site of a medieval iron smelting operation. High up to the east the Kinder River falls over the escarpment from the plateau to form Kinder Downfall, highest waterfall in the National Park.

On the Snake Path at Hayfield.

5 Now follow the path down the stone-walled fields to Tunstead Clough Farm.

6 Below this farm it is simply a matter of following the lane as it curves down to the wooded territory of the valley bottom where the infant River Sett comes in from the south (left). A short walk brings us back to the car park at Bowden Bridge.

4 Higher Shelf Stones and the Roman Road

Exploring Bleaklow's western slopes.

Level: 🥾 🥾 🥾
Length: 8.5 miles (12.5 kms)
Ascent: 1,550 feet (470 metres)
Terrain: Stiff moorland walking. Some rocky ground. Not advisable in low cloud.
Park & Start: Old Glossop. GR042947
Info: Heritage Centre in Glossop. Refreshments in Glossop.

This route climbs from the former mill town of Glossop, up the western flanks of Bleaklow, the largest area of wild country uncrossed by a public road and second only in altitude to Kinder Scout in the entire Peak District.

We visit one of Bleaklow's rockiest summits, Higher Shelf Stones, and view an aviation relic nearby. Then we continue along the line of the Pennine Way to pick up the Roman road (called Doctor's Gate)

originally constructed to connect the Roman fort at Brough in the Hope Valley and Melandra, just west of Glossop.

In the later stages of our route we follow the tumblings of the Shelf Brook in its beautiful moorland valley, past Mossy Lea, one of the largest hill farms in Peakland, and so back to that part of town called Old Glossop. This is a really rewarding, if fairly tough, walk through exposed high ground.

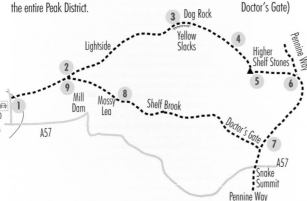

(1) From Old Glossop take the track that starts just below the church, heading west, and soon cross the boundary into the Peak District National Park.

(2) In less than a mile (1 km) follow the path on the left that heads up the slope and after one field cross the boundary into Open Country and so climb through Lightside, aiming for the broken edge called Yellow Slacks, keeping on the north side of the drystone wall with Dog Rock as the next goal.

(3) Dog Rock makes a good spot to rest and take in the wild view of open moorland and the craggy ground falling away from your feet to the Yellow Slacks Brook. Continue now up the gentle slope beside the drystone

The Shelf Brook below Mossylee Farm.

wall then keeping close to the diminutive trickle in shallow Dowstone Clough.

(4) Before gaining the watershed turn steadily towards the south, still ascending gradually towards the distant trig. pillar on the top of Higher Shelf Stones at 2,037 feet (621 metres). In clear conditions this rocky summit makes a super belvedere, allowing

prospects down the dale of the Shelf Brook to the sprawl of Glossop and beyond across part of Greater Manchester and across the Cheshire Plain.

(5) We are at the day's high point – there are only one or two tops on Bleaklow that rise a little higher than this. Before setting off on the second part of our route it is worth

The trackway that climbs the Ashop Valley from the east to then descend the valley of the Shelf Brook towards Glossop is called Doctor's Gate in its highest reaches 1,618 feet (512 metres) above sea level. It is the original Roman route linking Anavio (Brough) in the Hope Valley with Melandra beside the River Etherow west of Glossop. The paving we see today across the highest, bleakest part of the watershed (just north of the Snake Pass) is much more recent and is thought to have been paid for by Doctor John Talbot of Glossop, hence its name.

Moorside near Old Glossop.

Hollingworth Hall Moor from above Old Glossop.

Much of the worst bogland on this crossing has been made easier for walkers with pathway construction.

(7) Before reaching the Snake Pass highway the Pennine Way crosses the line of the Roman road called here Doctor's Gate. We

Glossop from Higher Shelf Stones.

going down a short way to the east to discover one of the major aircraft wrecks of the southern Pennines (see information panel on the right).

(6) Head east now to gain the beaten path which is the Pennine Way where it crosses Hern Clough. Now head south towards the distant top of the Snake Pass (A57).

At GR 090950 just east of Higher Shelf Stones summit is the crash site of a USAF Superfortress B29. This is the same class that was used to drop atomic bombs on Hiroshima and Nagasaki in 1945. This particular aircraft crashed here in November, 1948 en route from Scampton, Lincolnshire to the USAF base at Burtonwood, Warrington just before darkness fell. Low cloud caused it to fly into the topmost few feet of the summit and all thirteen crew members were killed. For some years all wreckage of the giant plane lay on the peaty surface but some of it was demolished and buried. Today erosion has revealed some of the wreck, making an interesting memorial to this tragic event.

turn right (west) along this and soon begin the steep descent into the clough (valley) of the Shelf Brook. In 2 miles (3 kms) the boundary of Open Country is gained and we now traverse the enclosed hill pastures of Mossy Lea Farm.

8 Continue straight down the valley, passing a former mill dam over to the left in the lee of shapely Shire Hill and soon rejoin our outward route.

9 Retrace steps down the track to return to Old Glossop.

Winter on the Bleaklow plateau.

5 **A Round of Eastern Bleaklow**

A moorland route near the source of the River Derwent.

Level: 🐾 🐾
Length: 6.25 miles (10 kms)
Ascent: 750 feet (230 metres)
Terrain: Steady valley walking and stiff moorland crossing.
Park & Start: King's Tree at road-head in upper Derwent Dale. GR 167939
Info: National Park Information Centre at Fairholmes downstream of Derwent Reservoir impounding wall. Also refreshments and cycle hire.

This 6 miles (9.5 kms) walk gives a flavour of wonderful upper Derwent Dale and the changes wrought here by man in the last 100 years. There is the open dale, forestry plantation, grouse moor and a feeling of freedom on the high gritstone territory on this eastern flank of Bleaklow.

Often called "Britain's only true desert" there are no palm-edged oases or dunes here; just a temperate desert of heather, moss and moor grasses covering the deep peat beds of former ancient forests.

Ideal for rearing grouse for sport shooting for many generations we can experience the silence and open skies beside the two shooting cabins in Lower Small Clough. Early in our walk we pass the site of old Ronksley Farm, swept away like others in the upper dale when the trio of giant reservoirs was constructed here from early in the twentieth century to supply the growing needs of Derby, Nottingham, Leicester and Sheffield.

At historic Slippery Stones the ancient packhorse bridge from Derwent village makes a useful and fascinating crossing point of the River Derwent, replacing the hazardous ford on the shelving gritsone slabs below.

Park at the King's Tree where the narrow public road from the lower dale has its ending.

 Walk north along the good track and cross the mouth of Lynch Clough at the ford just below the site of former Ronksley Farm. Head on up the track to Slippery Stones.

 Cross the lovely old packhorse bridge erected here in 1959 (see information panel) and turn left (north) to follow the dale's floor close to the young River Derwent for about 2 miles (3.25 kms).

Autumn in upper Derwent Dale.

Crow Stones Edge from Swine Side.

The Derwent Valley Water Board was established in 1899 to build three large reservoirs to supply Derby, Nottingham, Leicester and Sheffield. Howden Reservoir, the upper one, came into service in 1912 and Derwent Reservoir in 1916. Construction of the lowest, Ladybower, began in 1935 and was officially inaugurated by King George VI in 1945.

(4) Soon after passing the broad landslip called Deer Holes, seen directly across the river at high level, seek a crossing of the Derwent to access the lower end of Lower Small Clough and follow the tiny path up this shallow side valley that heads south-west towards the wild terrain of Ridgewalk Moor.

Oak and larch, October in Derwent Dale.

(5) In less than 1 mile (1.5 kms) we reach the secret site in the upper clough of a pair of shooting cabins. One was originally intended for the "guns" out for a day's grouse shooting in late summer and autumn, the other a more rudimentary affair for the beaters. This place makes an ideal refreshment break, especially in bad weather.

(6) Continue up to the shallow head of Lower Small Clough and pick out the old ditch called Black Dike which heads south-east down the gently sloping moor. In less than 1.5 miles (2.5 kms) turn left and soon descend the steeper slopes falling into Lynch Clough.

Right: Charollais store cattle, Derwent Dale.

7 Follow the floor of Lynch Clough downhill and pick up the tiny path that makes for easier progress and leave the Open Country into the plantation.

8 We are soon down near the site of Ronksley Farm and the ford. Cross this heading south and in a short distance reach our starting point at King's Tree.

Derwent Edge from Ladybower Reservoir.

Flooding of Derwent Dale behind the Ladybower impounding embankment meant the loss of the villages of Ashopton and Derwent. Lovely Derwent Hall was built in 1672 and in the early twentieth century was owned by the Duke of Norfolk. Before being demolished as the water rose towards it after 1935 oak panelling from the Hall was installed in the Derwent Valley Water Board's offices at Bamford.

The beautiful old packhorse bridge over the Derwent was taken down in 1938 and stored in a barn until re-erected in 1959 at Slippery Stones as a memorial to the great countryside campaigner John Derry.

The Derwent packhorse bridge, Slippery Stones.

6 The Wessenden Valley and West Nab

Wild country at the northern extremity of the National Park.

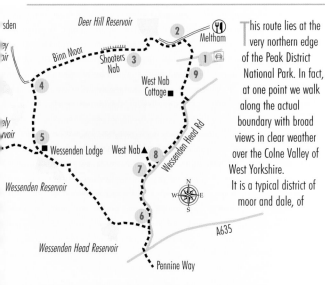

Level: 🥾 🥾
Length: 8 miles (12.5 kms)
Ascent: 1,200 feet (365 metres)
Terrain: Some rough moorland but some good paths and tracks.
Park & Start: Moorland lane west of Meltham, e.g. GR 089107
Info: Refreshments in Meltham.

This route lies at the very northern edge of the Peak District National Park. In fact, at one point we walk along the actual boundary with broad views in clear weather over the Colne Valley of West Yorkshire.

It is a typical district of moor and dale, of drystone walls and a string of reservoirs and reaches the notable high point of West Nab at 1,641 feet (500 metres) from where we have a wonderful prospect of the undulating hill farms that occupy much of this area to the south of Huddersfield.

① Park on one of the straight lanes almost a mile due west of Meltham church, say at New Bridge – GR089106. Walk west then take the footpath that heads off right (towards the north-west) and pick up the lane that soon gives access to Deer Hill Reservoir.

② Head up towards the reservoir and soon take the path to the left that climbs and curves up the moor towards Deer Hill and so cross the boundary into Open Country.

Deer Hill above Meltham.

③ Continue generally south-west, along the crest of the north-facing gritstone escarpment called Shooter's Nab, part of which is a former quarry. The name is associated with the rifle range that lies below (west of the reservoir) and the early climbers that explored these

Shooters Nab Quarry, above Meltham.

rocks in the mid-twentieth century "noted thoughtfully the numerous bullet holes in the rock faces !"

4 Beyond Shooter's Nab the land descends gently across Binn Moor to pick up a small stream that flows down to the head of Butterley Reservoir. We soon gain the level track that contours south up the windings of this Wessenden Valley.

5 Head south on this easy track, looking down as we go to Blakeley Reservoir, then Wessenden Reservoir. At the impounding wall of Wessenden Reservoir we join the revised main route of the Pennine Way which comes in from the west. Continue south along the track, passing the highest reservoir in this

In Short Grain, Wessenden Valley.

*View over West Yorkshire
from West Nab.*

West Nab is a remarkable viewpoint. The summit rises to
1,640 feet (500 metres) and gives wonderful vistas right
across West Yorkshire, including Emley Moor television tower
9.5 miles (15.25 kms) to the east-north-east and at 1,084 feet
(330 metres) is Britain's tallest unsupported tower. At a much
greater distance the towers of York Minster are visible in very
clear conditions.

valley — Wessenden Head Reservoir — and so up to the third class public road, Wessenden Head Road.

6 Turn left along Wessenden Head Road (the Pennine Way heads right).

7 Walk along the road for almost a mile (1.5 kms) with the rocky crest of West Nab ahead. At the highest point of the road, about 1,500 feet (457 metres), leave the road and make directly up to the top of West Nab for some fine views over West Yorkshire when conditions are clear.

All about this summit are eroded gritstone tors, not unlike better known ones on Bleaklow and Kinder Scout. One such tor here on West Nab was the ancient Rocking Stone but by 1827 it had been toppled by stone masons using wedges. A case of outright vandalism.

Summer at Wessenden Lodge.

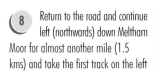

8 Return to the road and continue left (northwards) down Meltham Moor for almost another mile (1.5 kms) and take the first track on the left

that passes below West Nab Cottage. On reaching a block of woodland the track turns right but we continue on the path ahead and soon gain a lane.

9 Turn right down the lane, Brow Grains Road, towards Meltham and return to the starting point.

On West Nab.

7 Along the Pennine Way to Black Hill

A classic walk on one of Peakland's highest plateaux.

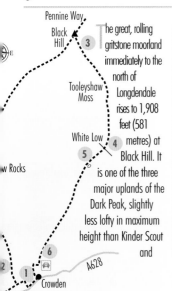

Level: 🥾 🥾 🥾
Length: 8.5 miles (13.5 kms)
Ascent: 1,230 feet (375 metres)
Terrain: Wild moorland, difficult to navigate in poor visibility. Good flagged path up to summit of Black Hill.
Park & Start: Crowden campsite and youth hostel. GR 073993

The great, rolling gritstone moorland immediately to the north of Longdendale rises to 1,908 feet (581 metres) at Black Hill. It is one of the three major uplands of the Dark Peak, slightly less lofty in maximum height than Kinder Scout and Bleaklow. Several major cloughs (valleys) cut into the southern flanks of Black Hill — Crowden Great Clough, Crowden Little Clough and Heyden Clough.

The Pennine Way climbs northwards from Crowden hamlet in Longdendale, rising high above the Crowden Great Brook to pass the gritstone crag of Laddow Rocks, scene of early pioneering climbing activity.

The great, wide dome of peaty moorland that is the top of Black Hill was notorious for its difficult underfoot going after wet weather. Alfred Wainwright noted that "it is not the only fell with a summit of peat, but no other shows such desolate and hopeless quagmire to the sky". Progress has certainly been made easier in recent years by the construction of a stone path using slabs from defunct West Yorkshire textile mills. The bare peat around the summit has been re-seeded so that heather, moor grasses and bilberry have re-colonised it to look much more attractive.

43

From the car park at Crowden, close to the youth hostel and campsite in Longdendale, make for the Pennine Way to the west of the Crowden Great Brook which

comes down from the high ground to run into the head of Torside Reservoir.

 Follow the Pennine Way north, climbing past Laddow Rocks.

Then less steeply on the improved path to the almost imperceptible bump of Dun Hill and so forward to the trig. point atop Black Hill at 1,908 feet (581 metres). The actual broad and peaty

Torside Reservoir, Longdendale.

Improving the Pennine Way on Black Hill.

summit waste is called Soldier's Lump (see information panel) and from here in clear conditions you can see the pencil-thin transmission mast on Holme Moss a mile (1.5 kms) to the south-east.

3 In mist take great care to head off from this featureless moortop, aiming south-east across Tooleyshaw Moss.

4 About 1.75 miles (2.75 kms) from Black Hill summit we gain the gentle top of White Low, still quite high at 1,739 feet (530 metres) above sea level.

The summit of Black Hill, looking to Holme Moss television mast.

On Pikenaze Moor, upper Longdendale.

The broad dome that is Black Hill summit is also known as Soldier's Lump because the Corps of Royal Engineers camped here in 1905 to survey and map the area. An earlier party of Royal Engineers had come here for the same purpose in 1784 using the impressive 36 inch Great Ramsden theodolite. Excavations here in 1841 revealed the framework timbers belonging to the important piece of survey equipment which, incidentally, is now housed at the Science Museum, South Kensington, London.

5 Take care here on this fairly featureless ground to turn towards the south-west across Westend Moss, skirting to the right (west) of a small pond then continue on a steepening slope down Hey Moss.

6 About 1.5 miles (2.5 kms) beyond the small pond the path has fallen to the broken ground of Hey Edge and we leave the Open Access territory to zigzag down to our starting point at Crowden.

The mouth of Crowden Great Brook from Highstone Rocks.

8 Chinley Churn, South Head and New Smithy

Hillside paths in the western Dark Peak.

Level: 🥾🥾
Length: 7.75 miles (12.5 kms)
Ascent: 920 feet (280 metres)
Terrain: Some rough hill country but a lot of easier paths through upland pastures.
Park & Start: Chinley, around GR 040826
Info: Refreshments in Chinley.

Here's a grand walk over hill country less serious than many in the Dark Peak. It's often the case that mid-height hills like these give better perspective views of the landscape than higher ones.

We set out from Chinley, once an important Midland Railway junction, and aim for the quarried east face of attractive Chinley Churn before rotating clockwise to take in shapely South Head, at 1,622 feet (494 metres) the highest point of this route, to return on pleasant paths passing hill farms typical of this part of the western Dark Peak.

[Map showing route with numbered points 1–8, features including Mount Famine, Chinley Head, South Head, Shireoaks, New Smithy, Chinley, and roads A624 and A62. Compass rose showing N-E-S-W orientation.]

1 At Chinley take the appropriately named Over Hill Road that heads north-west near the railway station and just beyond Dryclough Farm take the footpath to the right that climbs the slopes of Cracken Edge.

Chinley Churn from Eccles Pike.

Bagshaw village and Chinley Churn (right).

2 The official path doesn't go over the 1,480 feet (451 metres) top of Chinley Churn but continues through the old quarry workings once involved with the production of roof slates and paving slabs.

3 Continue on the path which passes behind Whiterakes Farm before curving round towards the east to reach the obvious col (Chinley Head) at Hills House (see information panel).

South Head from near Chapel en le Frith.

Bagshaw Hall near Chapel en le Frith.

Hills House stands at Chinley Head and is known locally as "Peep O'Day Farm" on account of the unusual eye-shaped first floor window. Facing east it admits the first light of dawn and it is said there's a connection with the Protestant group founded in Ulster in the eighteenth century called the Peep O'Day Boys as they carried out their operations at dawn.

4 Turn left along the main road (A624) for a short distance then take the path to the right that soon connects to the broad track that climbs from Hayfield. Turn right (south) along it and continue around the southern flank of Mount Famine to enter Open Country and reach the foot of South Head summit cone. You can climb to the 1,622 feet (494 metres) top of this shapely little hill for some broad views then return to the track on this north side.

5 Follow the rough track towards the south-east between drystone walls for almost a mile (1.5 kms) then take the path forking to the right, straight down to beautifully situated Shireoaks then turn right (west) to cross the fields all the way down to Breckhead.

Looking to Roych Clough from Eccles Pike.

6 Just beyond that we gain the narrow public lane. Turn right and in a very short distance take the path passing Gorsty Low to reach the A624 at New Smithy.

7 Turn left to pass under the railway bridge and immediately turn right along the B6062 road.

8 Walk along the B6062 road to Chinley — about 0.75 mile (1.25 kms).

Pear Tree Cottage, near Chinley.

9 On Hollingworth Hall Moor

An easy ramble with views of dramatic Longdendale.

Here is an interesting corner of Longdendale which can be explored in a simple circuit that starts and ends at Tintwistle on the busy trans-Pennine Woodhead road (A628). We are here at the edge of the high moors that extend eastwards to the watershed of the south Pennines where the Pennine Way connects the massifs of Bleaklow and Black Hill mentioned in earlier chapters here.

Our particular route swings round from Tintwistle in an anticlockwise direction to take in the valley of the Ogden Brook, hillside woodland and the eastern slopes of Hollingworth Hall Moor before dropping towards the old mill villages of Hollingworth and Hadfield at the mouth of huge, glen-like Longdendale.

Level:
Length: 4 miles (6.5 kms)
Ascent: 330 feet (100 metres)
Terrain: Lane and field walking with some hillside traversing.
Park & Start: Tintwistle, around GR 023973

1 Starting at Tintwistle walk north-west along Arnfield Lane to the ancient farm settlement of Arnfield.

2 Cross the fields on a gentle descent to cross the Ogden Brook at Devil's Bridge, a delightful picnic spot.

Longdendale from below Lees Hill.

Being a valuable hunting ground in Norman times the powerful Peverils had a lodge here on the site of the later Hollingworth Hall. It eventually evolved into a fine seventeenth century mansion with a dramatic eastwards view up the wild length of Longdendale. It was the seat of the de Hollingworth family and in Victorian times was the home of reclusive Robert de Hollingworth, said to have been a local magistrate with a reputation for leniency.

Tintwistle from above Old Glossop.

3 Climb up through the hillside wood at Lower Bank and cross in a south-west direction to reach the site of demolished Hollingworth Hall.

4 Continue along the drive for a few hundred metres then take a footpath that heads down near to a narrow strip of woodland aiming south-east near to Meadowbank Farm on the northernmost edge of Hollingworth village.

5 Turn left along the public lane that soon crosses Hollingworth Brook (really a continuation of Ogden Brook that we crossed at Devil's Bridge) with the dam wall of Arnfield Reservoir visible ahead.

6 Turn left along the A628 to pass Arnfield Reservoir then either fork left up the public lane to Crossgates Farm then turn right along Arnfield Lane back to Tintwistle, or keep along the busy A628 to Tintwistle.

Swineshaw Moor from Hollingworth Hall Moor.

Early summer near Hollingworth Hall.

The place had a chequered history after his death in 1865 and in 1943 was sold for £3,100 to Manchester Corporation Waterworks and, as was a common bad habit at that time, it was demolished to prevent "pollution" of the reservoirs in lower Longdendale. Incidentally, when this string of dams was completed in 1877 it was the largest expanse of artificial water in the world, and today supplies about 24 million gallons of water to Manchester every day.

Above Mottram-in-Longdendale.

Right: In Ogden Clough.

10 Exploring the Hope Woodlands

Ancient trackways in reservoir country.

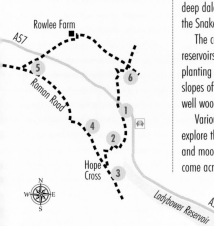

The Woodlands Valley is part of the valley drained by the River Ashop upstream of Ladybower Reservoir. The famous Snake Road (A57) uses the deep dale as it climbs west towards the Snake Pass and Greater Manchester.

The coming of the Derwent Valley reservoirs resulted in much forest planting so that today the lower slopes of the encircling hills are truly well wooded.

Various paths allow the walker to explore the valley floor, valley sides and moorland shoulders. Here we come across ruins of hill farms vacated

Level: 🐾 🐾
Length: 5 miles (8 kms)
Ascent: 880 feet (270 metres)
Terrain: Steep, wooded slopes and ancient trackways.
Park & Start: In lay-by beside A57 (Snake Road) at GR 164886.
Info: Refreshments at Fairholmes in Derwent Dale, at Bamford and at Hathersage.

to reduce pollution threats after the reservoirs were constructed; thriving bird life from heron to buzzard and, high up, the introduced red grouse. This really is delightfully varied gritstone hill country.

At Elmin Pitts Farm the family of Townsend lived. Joseph Townsend became one of the best known gamekeepers on these Chatsworth-owned grouse moors. Now the site of the old farm is a fern-covered ruin.

① Park in the lay-by beside the A57 Snake Road at GR 164886 and go down the track to the south to cross the bridge over the River Ashop.

② Cross the River Ashop on the convenient bridge and head upwards zigzag fashion through the mature plantation.

③ Climb out onto the track which is the original Roman route linking Navio in the Hope Valley with Melandra, near Glossop. Up here on the gentle ridge-top notice the old stone guide pillar called Hope Cross.

The site of Elmin Pitts Farm.

The tall, stone guide stone (or stoop) called Hope Cross marks the site of an older, medieval cross. It stands at the intersection of the Roman road that linked the Hope Valley fort of Navio (Brough) with the one near Glossop known as Melandra, and the packhorse track that climbs out of the Vale of Edale to descend into the Ashop Valley en route to upper Derwent Dale and Penistone beyond the high moors to the north. Hope Cross was restored in 1737.

4 Head north-west along the Roman road, gradually descending, for 1.5 miles (2.5 kms) until another ancient track comes up from Rowlee Bridge to the right.

The Roman road near Hope Cross.

Bradwell Edge from near Hope Cross.

(5) Turn down here, cross the bridge and climb the short distance to cross the Snake Road (A57) and continue uphill (north-east) past Rowlee Farm and keep on the track to ascend under rocky Pasture Tor and on by Bellhagg Barn to a crossroads of tracks near Woodcock Coppice.

(6) Turn down the track to the right, soon entering the woods and zigzag down to the A57, close to our starting point.

High above Derwent Dale.

This Hope Woodlands valley once had a much larger population than now. With the construction of Ladybower Reservoir during World War Two and its subsequent filling many of the scattered hill farms were abandoned for the usual reasons of pollution. High up above Rowlee Farm, at Bellhag Barn (mentioned in this walk's instructions) there was once a school that local children reached on foot from miles around in all weathers.

Exploring the Hope Woodlands

Late summer above the Ashop Valley.

Tributary of the River Ashop.